No part of this publication may be reproduced, distributed or transmitted in any form or by any means including photocopying, recording, or other electronic or mechanical methods, without the prior written permission of the publisher or author, except in the case of brief quotations embodied in critical reviews and certain other noncommercial uses permitted by copyright law. For permission requests, email the author at lisaabbott2016@gmail.com.

ISBN-13: 978-0-578-49757-0
Library of Congress Control Number: 2019916651
Ingramspark / Lightning Source, LaVergne, TX

Copyright © 2019 by Lisa Abbott

Be Kind to Your Mind

By Lisa Abbott
Illustrated by Sarah Fierle

Be kind to your mind by being *aware*.

Treat the thoughts and feelings you have with care.

Do not judge for they are neither wrong nor right.

Pay attention to them, and keep them in sight.

Be kind to your mind with each breath you take

To stay in the moment and stay awake.

Count each inhale and exhale to keep calm and cool,

If you're bothered about something at home or at school.

Be kind to your mind if you're nervous or stressed.

Maybe you're worried about taking a quiz or a test.

Grab some crayons and a coloring book.

Coloring will soon change your outlook.

Be kind to your mind, and learn to detach.

This will help when you're going through a rough patch.

Don't look to the future – forget about the past.

Think about now – slow down, make it last.

Be kind to your mind – be adventurous and explore.

Be engaged in what you love and adore.

Take pleasure in things both great and small.

This will help when you struggle or have a pitfall.

Be kind to your mind, and try to focus

On things that matter like spring's first crocus.

Look at its beauty, and take in its scent.

Paying attention to what matters is time well spent.

Be kind to your mind, and show gratitude.

For when you are grateful, it helps your mood.

Forget what you don't have – be thankful and giving.

Think about how to help others to make life worth living.

Be kind to your mind by opening your heart.

Listening to your inner voice is a good place to start.

How do you feel? What does it say?

What will your heart tell you today?

Be kind to your mind – let your imagination soar.

Take time to dream dreams you must not ignore.

Your mind is so powerful in what it can create,

So start imagining what you want, and don't leave it to fate.

Dear Journal,
    Today was a good day!

Be kind to your mind – put your thoughts in a place.

Write them down in a journal you cannot erase.

When you're angry, upset, frustrated or sad,

Writing things down helps them seem not as bad.

Be kind to your mind, and give Kudos when you can

To someone you don't know well or your biggest fan.

Compliments are gifts that are totally free.

Giving them feels good - I'm sure you'll agree.

Be kind to your mind, and laugh more, not less.

Laughter has been proven to reduce levels of stress.

It releases endorphins which make you feel good,

And helps your immune system work as it should.

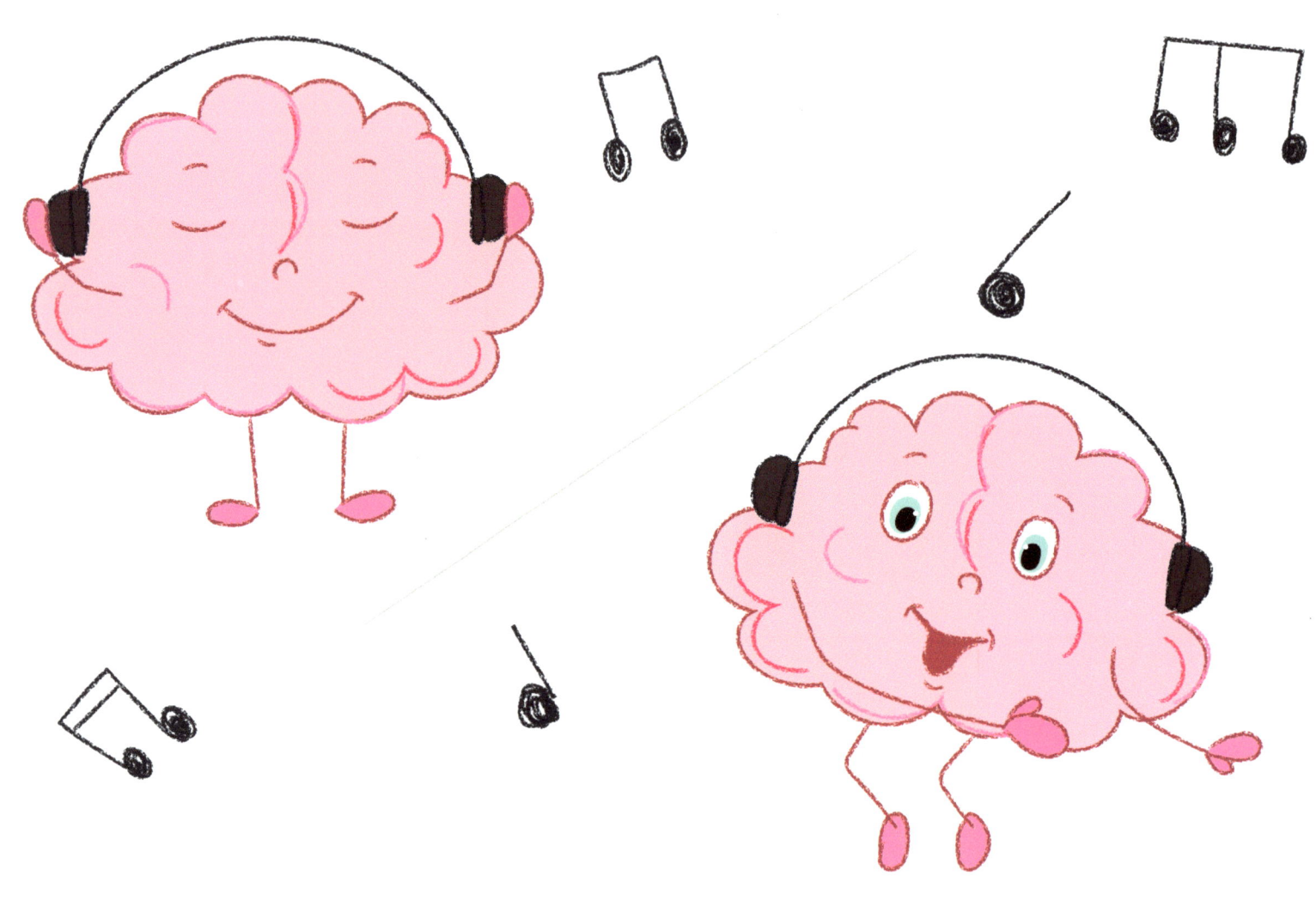

Be kind to your mind, and add music to your day.

It can help you relax when you work or play.

If you're feeling anxious, it will relieve your worry.

It also motivates you to get things done in a hurry.

Be kind to your mind, and give nature your attention.

There are so many great things about nature to mention.

Seeing the beauty of a flower, or resting under shady trees,

Or hearing the song of a bird can put your mind at ease.

Be kind to your mind – keep your thoughts open not shut.

New perspectives will prevent you from getting in a rut.

Being open-minded can allow you new ways

Of solving life's problems on your toughest of days.

Be kind to your mind, and have a place to go

When you need to be calm or are feeling quite low.

Count each and every blessing one by one.

Soon you'll feel ready to go get things done.

Be kind to your mind – take some time to be quiet.

You'll never know how nice it feels till you try it.

Escape from the noise – give distractions a rest.

Finding some peace will help you feel your best.

Be kind to your mind – reflect and think.

Savor the time because it's gone in a wink.

Think about today's highs, and was there a low?

Reflecting on the day will help your mind grow.

Be kind to your mind, and make your body be Still.

The only motion is your lungs that empty and fill.

Concentrate on not moving your hands or your feet.

The tranquility you feel is a wonderful treat.

Be kind to your mind, and use your sense of touch

When life gets hard and seems like too much.

Feel the warmth of the sun or a cool, gentle breeze.

Find someone you love and get a hug and a squeeze.

Be kind to your mind, and understand stress.

Too much is not good you probably would guess.

But having a little is a good motivator.

Try to find the right balance sooner not later.

Be kind to your mind, and learn to visualize.

This helps solve problems no matter what size.

Focus on a goal and the things you must do.

Picture the solution to make it come true.

Be kind to your mind, and take time to wonder.

Ask questions to learn if there's pressure you're under.

Wanting to know things will keep your brain strong.

Knowledge is power, so you can't go wrong.

Be kind to your mind and e✗ercise.

Getting extra oxygen to your brain is very wise.

Cells get repaired – learning and memory improve,

So put on your sneakers and get in your groove.

Be kind to your mind, and try yoga for fun.

You'll be more relaxed and calm when you're done.

It focuses on breathing to make your mind clear,

And positive thinking, so there's nothing to fear.

Be kind to your mind, and fill your life with zest.

Be enthusiastic each day, and give it your best.

Be mindful of the gifts life sends your way.

Feel emotion, have purpose and live for today.

www.ingramcontent.com/pod-product-compliance
Lightning Source LLC
Chambersburg PA
CBHW041154290426
44108CB00002B/70